AUG -- 2020
STARK LIBRARY

Blastoff! Readers are carefully developed by literacy experts to build reading stamina and move students toward fluency by combining standards-based content with developmentally appropriate text.

 **Level 1** provides the most support through repetition of high-frequency words, light text, predictable sentence patterns, and strong visual support.

 **Level 2** offers early readers a bit more challenge through varied sentences, increased text load, and text-supportive special features.

 **Level 3** advances early-fluent readers toward fluency through increased text load, less reliance on photos, advancing concepts, longer sentences, and more complex special features.

★ **Blastoff! Universe**

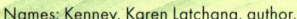

This edition first published in 2021 by Bellwether Media, Inc.

No part of this publication may be reproduced in whole or in part without written permission of the publisher. For information regarding permission, write to Bellwether Media, Inc., Attention: Permissions Department, 6012 Blue Circle Drive, Minnetonka, MN 55343.

Library of Congress Cataloging-in-Publication Data

Names: Kenney, Karen Latchana, author.
Title: Howler monkeys / by Karen Latchana Kenney.
Description: Minneapolis, MN : Bellwether Media, 2021. | Series: Blastoff! readers. Animals of the rain forest | Includes bibliographical references and index. | Audience: Ages 5-8 | Audience: Grades K-1 | Summary: "Relevant images match informative text in this introduction to howler monkeys. Intended for students in kindergarten through third grade"-- Provided by publisher.
Identifiers: LCCN 2019059313 (print) | LCCN 2019059314 (ebook) | ISBN 9781644872246 (library binding) | ISBN 9781618919823 (ebook)
Subjects: LCSH: Howler monkeys--Juvenile literature. | Rain forest animals--Juvenile literature.
Classification: LCC QL737.P915 K46 2021 (print) | LCC QL737.P915 (ebook) | DDC 599.8/55--dc23
LC record available at https://lccn.loc.gov/2019059313
LC ebook record available at https://lccn.loc.gov/2019059314

Text copyright © 2021 by Bellwether Media, Inc. BLASTOFF! READERS and associated logos are trademarks and/or registered trademarks of Bellwether Media, Inc.

Editor: Betsy Rathburn   Designer: Brittany McIntosh

Printed in the United States of America, North Mankato, MN

Table of Contents

Life in the Rain Forest 4
Stay Away! 10
Tree Eaters 16
Glossary 22
To Learn More 23
Index 24

Life in the Rain Forest

brown howler monkey

Howler monkeys are **primates**. They live across Central and South America.

These **mammals** have long arms and legs. These help the monkeys move through the rain forest **biome**!

Brown Howler Monkey Range

The rain forest is full of trees. Howler monkeys easily travel through them.

prehensile tail

The monkeys have **prehensile** tails. They can **grip** branches!

Rain forests are noisy! Howler monkeys must be loud to stand out.

Special Adaptations

special throat bones

prehensile tail

long arms and legs

The monkeys have special bones in their throats. This helps them make deep sounds!

Stay Away!

black-and-gold howler monkeys

The rain forest is full of **predators**.

Howler monkeys form **troops** to stay safe. Troops have up to 20 monkeys!

troop

Howler monkey troops avoid other troops. They **defend** their **territories**.

Venezuelan red howler monkeys

They howl to keep other monkeys away. They mark their branches with **dung** piles!

If another troop comes near, male howler monkeys attack.

They scream loudly. They jump and bite. This scares the other troop away!

Brown Howler Monkey Stats

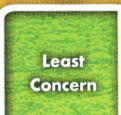

Least Concern	Near Threatened	Vulnerable	Endangered	Critically Endangered	Extinct in the Wild	Extinct

conservation status: least concern

life span: up to 20 years

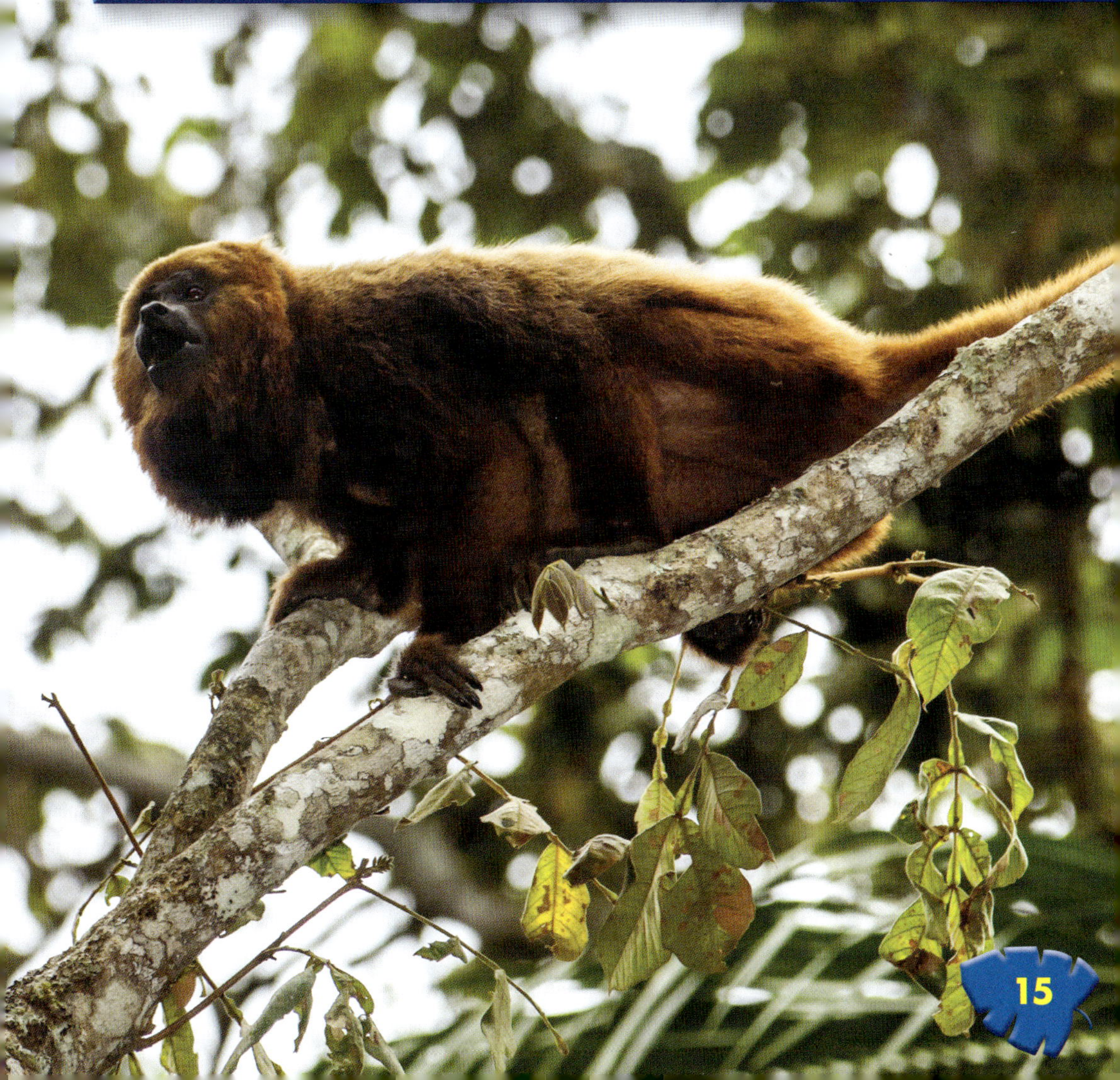

Tree Eaters

Howler monkeys find food in the rain forest **canopy**. They mostly eat leaves.

The monkeys also eat flowers, fruits, and nuts. Sharp **molars** help them chew tough foods!

Howler Monkey Diet

cashews

papaya

shortleaf fig leaves

The monkeys drop seeds in their dung. The seeds fall to forest floor.

mantled howler monkey

Soon, new plants sprout. Howler monkeys help the rain forest grow!

Howler monkeys **thrive** in busy rain forests. They have **adapted** to find food and stay safe.

Their howls **echo** throughout the rain forest!

Glossary

adapted—changed over a long period of time

biome—a large area with certain plants, animals, and weather

canopy—the uppermost level of the rain forest

defend—to protect someone or something from being harmed

dung—poop

echo—to make a sound that repeats; an echo is caused by sound waves bouncing off of objects and back to the listener.

grip—to hold tightly

mammals—warm-blooded animals that have backbones and feed their young milk

molars—large teeth at the back of the mouth

predators—animals that hunt other animals for food

prehensile—able to grip

primates—animals that use their hands to grasp food and other objects; primates are related to humans.

territories—land areas where animals live

thrive—to grow well

troops—groups of howler monkeys that live and eat together

To Learn More

AT THE LIBRARY
Grack, Rachel. *Chimpanzees*. Minneapolis, Minn.: Bellwether Media, 2019.

Huddleston, Emma. *Looking into the Rain Forest*. Mankato, Minn.: The Child's World, 2020.

Silen, Andrea. *Rainforests*. Washington, D.C.: National Geographic Kids, 2020.

ON THE WEB

FACTSURFER

Factsurfer.com gives you a safe, fun way to find more information.

1. Go to www.factsurfer.com.
2. Enter "howler monkeys" into the search box and click 🔍.
3. Select your book cover to see a list of related content.

Index

adaptations, 9, 20
arms, 5, 9
attack, 14
biome, 5
branches, 7, 13
canopy, 16
Central America, 4
defend, 12
dung, 13, 18
echo, 21
food, 16, 17, 20
grip, 7
howl, 13, 21
legs, 5, 9
males, 14
mammals, 5
molars, 17
plants, 19
predators, 10
prehensile tails, 7, 9

primates, 4
range, 4, 5
scream, 14
seeds, 18
sounds, 9
South America, 4
status, 15
territories, 12
throats, 9
travel, 6
trees, 6
troops, 11, 12, 14

The images in this book are reproduced through the courtesy of: reisegraf.ch, front cover; Leonardo Mercon, pp. 4, 15; Sandra Padinger, p. 6; spatuletail, p. 7; Anton_Ivanov, pp. 8, 23; Milan Zygmunt, p. 9; FLPA/ Age Fotostock, p. 10; Urs Hauenstein/ Alamy, p. 11; blickwinkel/ Alamy, p. 12; Piotr Naskrecki/ Age Fotostock, p. 13; Diana Rebman/ Alamy p. 14; HT-Pix, p. 16; thanin kliangsa-ard, p. 17 (cashews); fotorawin, p. 17 (papayas); Karuna Eberl, p. 17 (shortleaf fig leaves); Tanguy de Saint-Cyr, p. 18; Oliver Lambert, p. 19; THPStock, p. 20; Octavio Campos Salles/ Alamy, p. 21.